CANINE DIABETES HANDBOOK

CANINE DIABETES HANDBOOK

Dan Lavach, DVM, MS, DACVO

EYE CARE FOR ANIMALS
9720 S. VIRGINA ST., STE. D
RENO, NEVADA 89511

To order additional copies of this book, contact:
Xlibris LLC
1-888-795-4274
www.Xlibris.com
Orders@Xlibris.com
142356

TABLE OF CONTENTS

INTRODUCTION

So, your dog has diabetes? So does mine. I was in shock and distressed when my dog Scout became acutely ill and almost died. She recovered from her acute illness thanks to great veterinary care provided by the Animal Emergency Clinic in Reno, but she went on to develop diabetes. I know what you are going through! Diabetes has become an epidemic disease in dogs and people. **Diabetes in dogs has increased by an estimated 32% during the previous ten years**. As a veterinary ophthalmologist I have examined and treated hundreds of diabetic patients. This handbook has been written to help you understand canine diabetes. It will not answer every question, but it will give you sufficient information to begin to understand the causes, mechanisms, and treatments available for diabetic dogs. This handbook will help you understand your veterinarian's recommendations and concerns for you and your pet. You will need to become a good observer about your pet's lifestyle and activities so you can accurately report information to your veterinarian. Diabetes can be well regulated in most affected dogs, while others dogs will have ups and downs, and more intensive care will be necessary. Don't give up if you feel overwhelmed at first. You were probably not trained to give injections and understand diseases, but with a little effort, you can become an excellent caretaker for you friend, your pet. Diabetic dogs can live long and happy lives; they just need a little more care than a non-diabetic pet. This handbook will begin with some general background information about normal metabolism. Additional sections will discuss causes of diabetes, treating diabetes, and complications associated with diabetes. Treating your diabetic pet will cause you and your pet to become closer than you can imagine. Don't be discouraged by setbacks; try to understand why your pet might be having difficulties. You and your veterinarian can figure it out! Good Luck!

NORMAL CANINE METABOLISM

Healthy dogs have an amazing ability to digest and utilize nutrients from a wide range of food sources. Both cooked and raw meats and vegetables can provide healthy food sources. Raw foods are at risk for bacterial contamination, and dogs can become infected from eating uncooked contaminated food. Cooked or prepared foods can spoil if not properly stored, causing disease in healthy dogs. Raw food and home cooked meals need to be stored and carefully prepared to prevent illness.

Dogs do not have enzymes in the saliva aiding in digestion. Canine saliva is primarily water with about 1% mucin. Saliva acts as a lubricant during chewing and swallowing. Saliva increases fluid mixing in the stomach and intestines. Chewing food breaks down large particles into smaller components, aiding in digestion. During digestion a normal dog breaks down complex foods into organic compounds in the stomach and small intestine. Stomach acid in the dog has a much lower pH than human stomach acid. This stronger acid is efficient in breaking down food and preparing it for digestion. This partially explains how dogs can digest food without "properly chewing their food". The digested food is absorbed in the small intestine, and it is delivered to the liver for processing. The pancreas is located next to the stomach and small intestine. The pancreas secretes digestive enzymes into the intestine to help in digestion of proteins. In addition, the pancreas secretes a hormone, insulin, into the blood. Basal insulin production by the normal pancreas provides a continuous level of insulin that remains in the blood at all times. Basal insulin production aids in maintaining healthy blood sugar levels throughout the day. Bolus insulin production occurs when a large bursts of insulin has been released into the blood. Bolus insulin production is usually associated following a meal or ingestion of a large sugar load.

Insulin helps mobilize blood glucose into all body cells. Glucose is the necessary fuel to keep all cells working and healthy. Insulin helps the body build and store glycogen (carbohydrates), fats, and proteins. Insulin reduces the breakdown of stored glycogen, fats, and protein. **Insufficient insulin production results in diabetes mellitus, commonly reported as simply diabetes.**

WHAT ARE THE RISK FACTORS OR CAUSES FOR DIABETES?

Diabetic dogs are primarily affected with a form of type-1 diabetes similar to latent autoimmune diabetes of adult humans (LADA)[1]. Diabetes can be acquired in any dog as a result of pancreatitis and destruction of the insulin producing cells in the pancreas. Evidence of acute or chronic pancreatitis occurs in about 40% of diabetic dogs, although many affected dogs never had signs of pancreatitis[2]. Diabetes can be a familial disease with a genetic basis[4]. The genetic abnormality may need to be activated by dietary or environmental factors.

Diabetes is more common in middle age and older dogs, especially if they are overweight. High carbohydrate diets and lack of exercise contribute to developing diabetes. Similarly, high fat diets and lack of exercise can cause increased weight gain and contribute to causing diabetes. High fat diets also reduce the efficiency of insulin uptake from blood plasma into the brain, so the brain becomes deficient in insulin[3]. If the brain is deficient in insulin, it cannot utilize glucose properly, the brain will stimulate an increase in hunger, contributing to weight gain. High fat diets also reduce insulin sensitivity in the peripheral tissues and, again, favors weight gain[3]. High fat diets potentially increase the risks for pancreatitis and subsequently diabetes[4]. Thus, poor diets and obesity can contribute to causing diabetes. In summary, high carbohydrate diets, lack of exercise, and obesity are absolutely related to causing diabetes in many pet dogs.

Certain dog breeds are more susceptible to diabetes, but the reason for this increased risk is not understood. In the past five years I have examined 5542 dogs. Diabetes and eye diseases related to diabetes were found in 258 dogs; this is approximately 4.7% of the local dog population. A chart depicting the affected dog breeds can be found in the Appendix I. The breed susceptibility for diabetes will vary with the distribution of breeds in different geographic areas

Insulin is the primary therapy for diabetic dogs. Most diabetic dogs require twice-daily dosing with insulin to control clinical signs.

Once a dog develops diabetes, it will need lifelong insulin treatments. Strict diet control will be important to control diabetes, and routine exercise will be beneficial.

WHAT ARE THE SIGNS
OF DIABETES?

Dogs affected with diabetes usually have a sudden onset of clinical signs including the following: increased thirst and water consumption (polydipsia), increased urination (polyuria), loss of bladder control, (the urine becomes sticky because of the high sugar content in diabetic's urine), increased appetite, rapid weight loss, lethargy, and weakness. If diabetes is not recognized, the dog will become progressively weaker, and the appetite will become suppressed. Secondary infections especially urinary tract infections, dental disease, and skin diseases are common in diabetic dogs. **Cataracts progressing to blindness always occur in diabetic dogs. The cataracts can occur very early in the disease and very quickly.** Cataracts can develop within 3-4 days, causing sudden blindness. Peripheral neuropathies can develop in diabetic dogs. The signs of a peripheral neuropathy are variable depending what part of the nervous system is affected. Peripheral neuropathies represent nerve injuries. Poor circulation and high blood sugar levels cause neuropathies. In diabetic humans, nerve injuries manifest as a tingling or local intermittent pain, but it can progress to chronic pain and/or eventually loss of all sensation. Similar sensations probably occur in dogs. A few examples of peripheral nerve damage in dogs might include intermittent or chronic limping, signs of pain in the leg(s), loss of eyelid blinking, reduced tear production, and hypersensitivity to touch portions of the skin. The autonomic nerves (involuntary part of the nervous system controlling body function such as heart rate, intestinal movements, etc.) can develop neuropathies. Autonomic neuropathies can affect heart muscle function, blood pressure, bowel movement, hair growth, etc.

HOW DOES DIABETES AFFECT THE EYES?

A brief description of the anatomy of the eye and how the normal eye functions will increase the understanding about the effects of diabetes on the eye. The outer shell of the eye is comprised of the clear cornea and the white sclera. The clear cornea is colorless and functions like a windshield on a car. Light travels through the cornea and passes through a clear fluid filled chamber, the anterior chamber. Light then passes through the pupil; the pupil is a dark space, not really an object. The pupil is similar to the dark opening to a cave or tunnel. The normal healthy lens fills the pupil zone, but it cannot be seen without special lighting because it too is clear and colorless. Light passes through the lens into the clear vitreous gel behind the lens. Light travels through the vitreous, finally into the retina where it begins the complex reactions that will be completed in the brain and produce vision.

THE CORNEA

The cornea is the clear window covering of the eye. The cornea has more sensory nerve endings than any other tissue in the body. It is very sensitive to touch, and the sensitivity helps protect the cornea by stimulating blinking and tearing when the cornea nerves are irritated. The cornea is also a special tissue because it does not have a blood supply. The cornea derives its nutrition from the tear film and the aqueous (clear fluid) inside the anterior chamber.

A small amount of glucose is present in the tear film of healthy dogs. Normal tear fluid contains water, Vitamin A and other nutrients, lubricating oils, mucus, and protective enzymes and chemicals. The tear film is very important in maintaining the health of the surfaces of the eye (cornea and conjunctivae). Tear glucose levels can become elevated in diabetes resulting in a favorable culture medium for bacteria. Increased populations of bacteria living in the conjunctival sac and on the ocular surfaces can cause conjunctivitis and/or spontaneous ulceration of the cornea. Diabetic dog corneas tend to lack normal sensitivity[3]. In addition, diabetic dogs often have lower tear production and less stable tear films resulting in dry eyes[5]. Decreased cornea sensitivity reduces tear production and eyelid blinking, so tears are not properly distributed across the cornea surface. The eyelids may tend to be partly open when the dog is asleep, and this causes increased drying of the ocular surfaces. Cornea ulcerations in diabetic dogs are caused by poor tear quality/quantity, poor eyelid blinking, infections, and poor nerve stimulation to promote normal cell growth and healing. Cornea ulcers in diabetic dogs are often complicated by prolonged healing times. Aggressive medical and/or surgical treatment can be vital in preventing serious complications in ulcerated corneas. People with diabetes experience similar risks for infections and slowly healing ulcers and wounds.

Diabetic dogs often have elevated blood levels of cholesterol and triglycerides (fats). The fats can leak into the cornea, causing mild to moderate clouding of the cornea. The exact mechanism for fats to leak into the cornea is not clearly known, but inflammation of blood vessels can allow fats to escape into surrounding tissues. As the fats accumulate in the cornea they cause a haze to form. Severe clouding of the cornea will reduce vision clarity. Unfortunately, this is a difficult problem to control. Medications (statins) useful in lowering cholesterol in humans are not effective in dogs. Increased fiber in the diet, reevaluation of the diet, and controlling inflammation in the eye may be the best methods to limit cornea clouding by lipids (fats).

THE AQUEOUS

The aqueous is the normal colorless, clear fluid filling the front part of the eye (anterior chamber). Aqueous is derived from blood that is passing through the ciliary body. Special cells lining the surface of the ciliary body, the ciliary epithelium, allow water from blood and substances dissolved in water to flow into the eye, first into the posterior chamber, then forward through the pupil, and then into the anterior chamber. The aqueous with its contents are important sources of nutrition for the lens and cornea. The lens and cornea lack blood vessels, so these two privileged tissues depend upon normal flow of aqueous for nutrition. The fluid does not normally contain large proteins, cells, or fats, but glucose, sodium, potassium, and substances that can be dissolved in water will pass into the anterior chamber. This fluid is referred to as aqueous or aqueous humor because of its water base.

The aqueous exits the anterior chamber through a complex network of cells and channels that ultimately deliver the aqueous back into the venous blood supply. This drain system is located at the junction of the cornea with the sclera and the root or base of the iris. It is not visible without using specialized examination techniques. The process of aqueous production and drainage is constantly in action in healthy eyes, and it is the balance between production and drainage that results in variations in pressure in the eye (intraocular pressure or IOP). The normal eye has a range of pressure that is acceptable for providing sufficient nutrition to the cornea and lens. If intraocular pressure is too high, the eye has glaucoma. If intraocular pressure is too low, inflammation or damage to the production area has occurred. Both low and high pressures are dangerous for the eye.

Abnormal contents in the aqueous can interfere with the health of the lens and cornea. Diabetic dogs typically have abnormally high glucose, cholesterol, and triglyceride levels in their blood. The fats (cholesterol, triglycerides, and esters) can contribute to local inflammation in the eye, and fats can leak into the aqueous. Clouding of the aqueous with fat contamination can obscure the pupil. Fat contamination in the aqueous and inflammatory products can obstruct drainage of aqueous out of the eye, resulting in glaucoma.

THE LENS

In diabetes, the amount of glucose in the blood is abnormally high, and this high level of glucose passes into the aqueous along with normal ingredients.

As excess glucose spills into the aqueous, the glucose begins to accumulate in the lens. In diabetic dogs the normal absorption and utilization of glucose by chemical reactions in the lens is altered. Excess glucose levels in the aqueous overwhelms the normal chemical reaction between glucose and the enzyme hexokinase in the lens. The chemical breakdown of glucose shifts to an alternative reaction utilizing the enzyme aldose reductase. Aldose reductase converts excess glucose into sorbitol. Sorbitol is an alcohol, and it cannot cross cell membranes or escape from the lens fibers. The formation and accumulation of sorbitol causes water to be absorbed into the lens from the aqueous resulting in lens swelling, rupturing of the lens fibers, and clouding of the lens. This clouding of the lens is cataract formation. This process of chemical reactions causing cataracts can be compared to cooking a fresh egg. A freshly opened egg will have a clear "white" around the yoke, and the clear white turns to solid white when it is cooked. This change from clear to solid white is caused by heat degrading the protein in the egg white. When the diabetic lens becomes white because of cataract, the lens protein has similarly become degraded, but the process was a chemical reaction rather than heat induced.

Blindness caused by cataract formation eventually occurs in diabetic dogs. Cataract formation seems to occur in well-controlled diabetics as well as those not well controlled. Even the well-controlled diabetics tend to have glucose levels that spike, and this eventually causes cataract formation. Canine diabetic population survey findings suggest most diabetic dogs will develop cataracts within 5-6 months from the diagnoses of diabetes[6].

The rapid and extreme swelling of the diabetic cataract can cause the lens to rupture, releasing large volumes of lens protein and debris into the aqueous in front of the lens and/or into the vitreous gel behind the lens. The contamination of the aqueous and/or vitreous with lens protein results in inflammation. This process (lens induced uveitis or LIU) results in rapid and intense inflammation, completely destroying the eye within a few days if not recognized and treated. Intense inflammation without lens capsule rupture can occur as the degraded protein from the cataractous lens fibers leak through the lens capsule back out into the ocular fluids (aqueous and vitreous). The inflammation associated with lens protein leakage can quickly progress to cause hemorrhage into the eye, adhesion formation between the lens and iris or cornea and iris, glaucoma, lens luxation, and destruction of the eye.

Longstanding diabetic cataracts tend to slowly leak toxic lens protein fluid out of the cataractous lens into the aqueous, resulting in chronic low-grade inflammation and slight shrinkage in the size of the cataractous lens. The smaller lens size and destruction of the supporting zonular ligaments can allow the lens to become displaced either forward into the anterior chamber or backwards into the vitreous. Or, the lens might push forward, pushing the iris forward without actually slipping in front of the pupil (iris). Even without displacement of the lens, chronic low-grade inflammation often causes secondary glaucoma because of damage to the outflow drain system and adhesion formation.

CATARACT SURGERY

Diabetics should have a complete ophthalmic examination as soon as diabetes has been diagnosed. This initial examination will provide baseline information about the eye while the lens is still clear, and the view of the deep eye tissues (retina and optic nerve) is still possible. Once cataracts have clouded the lens, the deep tissues will not be able to be seen. Treatment with anti-inflammatory eye medications will often be necessary in diabetic dogs. Treatments can prevent or reduce many complications of diabetes in the eyes, but cataracts will develop in all dogs with diabetes.

Eyes with controlled inflammation are usually suitable for cataract removal surgery. The veterinary ophthalmologist will determine if the eyes are suitable for cataract removal surgery. The ophthalmologist will work with your pet's veterinarian to coordinate care during the preoperative and postoperative periods. Cataract surgery is performed after the patient has become stable and insulin treatments are controlling blood glucose levels. Nevertheless, some diabetic dogs are very difficult to become completely regulated, and surgery might be performed despite perfect glucose regulation. If the eyes continue to deteriorate from inflammation associated with rapid cataract formation, surgery would be considered. Generally the surgical candidate will not be gaining or losing weight; thirst, water consumption, and urine production should not be excessive. Presurgical laboratory testing often includes a complete blood count (CBC), blood chemistry panel, thyroid function testing, glucose curve, and fructosamine testing. Special ophthalmic testing of the eye including measuring intraocular pressure, gonioscopy, ultrasonography, and electroretinography might be recommended as part of the screening process prior to considering surgery.

Long hair dogs should be bathed and groomed prior to surgery, because grooming will be limited until the cataract surgery incisions have healed. Dogs with dental problems should have dental treatments prior to cataract surgery, or dentistry will need to be delayed at least two months after cataract surgery. This reduces the risks of infection from the mouth spreading into the eyes.

Diabetic cataracts form in both eyes at the same time or very close to the same time. Surgery to remove both cataractous lenses is usually preferred at the same time rather than requiring two surgical procedures. Removal of both cataracts at the same time reduces the potential for inflammation caused by leaving a cataractous lens in one eye which can stimulate inflammation in the fellow eye. Nevertheless, the decision to operate on one or both eyes depends upon many factors, and the ophthalmologist will advise you of the best treatment recommendation.

Prior to surgery, the patient will be receiving medications to reduce inflammation and to prepare the eye for surgery. The ophthalmologist will advise you about feeding and insulin treatments to be given on the day of surgery. Follow the directions correctly!

The patient will have general anesthesia during surgery. The eyelashes will be trimmed, and long hair on the face around the eyes might be trimmed. One or more sites on the legs will be trimmed to provide a site for intravenous catheter placement. This will allow easy access when intravenous medications and fluids are administered. The dog will be position on the surgery table with the eye in an upward position. A surgical operating microscope will be positioned over the eye. The microscope magnifies the surgery field and aids in viewing the tissues in the eye and in suturing the incision site at the end of surgery. Once the eye is properly positioned and prepared for surgery, a small incision is made through the cornea at the top of the eye. A clear thick fluid described as a viscoelastic substance is infused into the anterior chamber. This fluid helps coat and protect the surfaces of the delicate eye tissues. A small incision is created in the cataractous lens capsule. The lens capsule is similar to a plastic wrap around the lens. This incision is extended in a circular fashion to remove a portion of the lens capsule. This is similar to creating an open window into the cataract. Once the window has been opened, a surgical instrument designed for cataract removal is inserted into the eye. The instrument, a phacoemulsifier, is a hand held device that infuses fluid into the eye and vacuums an equal volume out of the eye at the same time. This causes a flow of fluid at the tip of the instrument. The lining sleeve in the phacoemulsifier produces vibrations in the range of 30,000-60,000 times each second. The vibration creates ultrasonic energy, similar to the type of ultrasound used in teeth cleaning. The ultrasonic energy breaks up the cataract into small pieces. The cataract pieces are mixed with the circulating fluid and vacuumed out of the eye. When the ultrasonic action ("phaco"), irrigation, and aspiration procedure have removed the cataractous lens from its capsule, the first phase of surgery has been completed. This will leave an empty envelope or capsular bag that was previously occupied by the cataractous lens. Next, the cornea incision is slightly increased in size to allow an artificial lens to be implanted into the empty lens capsular bag. The viscoelastic substance is vacuumed from the anterior chamber. The cornea incision is sutured closed with small ophthalmic suture. The anterior chamber is reformed with sterile fluid, and an air bubble might be placed into the anterior chamber. The air bubble will quickly be absorbed out of the anterior chamber within 2-3 days, and it will help maintain normal pressure within the eye. Local injections of antibiotic and anti-inflammatory drugs might be administered beneath the conjunctiva of the eye at the completion of surgery. When the patient has awakened from anesthesia, a protective collar will be placed to prevent the pet from rubbing at the eye, causing inflammation and injury to the eye. This collar might be removed within a few days, or it might be left on for several weeks. **The length of time necessary for the collar depends upon the pet and his or her desire to rub at the eyes**.

Your home nursing care after surgery is very important! Application of eye drops, eye ointments, and oral medications are all given for very good medical reasons, and proper medication will reduce the risks for post-operative complications. If you have any questions about providing treatments, contact the doctor immediately. The typical cataract patient will have several examinations during the healing period, and home care treatments will be adjusted as needed. Regardless, most dogs show signs of improved vision within a few days, and vision will usually continue to improve during the first 4-6 weeks after surgery.

Complications of diabetic cataract removal surgery do not occur any more often than in non-diabetic dogs having cataract surgery[7]. Nevertheless, infections, glaucoma, and retinal detachments can occur after surgery. The cataractous lens might be poorly supported by the zonular ligaments in the eye. If the lens is poorly supported, an artificial lens may not be placed within the eye during surgery. The eye without an artificial lens will have poorer vision because it will not have a lens to focus light, and it will lack the normal light gathering ability of a lens. Unfortunately, the eye with poor ligament support may not have visible signs of this potential complication until during surgery. This type of complication is especially common as a genetic disorder in Jack Russell and other Terrier dogs, but it can occur in any breed. Eyes with longstanding cataracts have higher risks for poorly supported lenses due to low-grade inflammation and lens support ligament damage.

The lens capsule envelope holding the artificial lens usually shrinks around the artificial lens and secures the lens in place. Mild to moderate clouding of the capsule is common; however, this clouding does not usually cause signs of vision impairment. Laser treatments to reduce capsule clouding or to create small windows in the capsule usually do not result in signs of vision improvement. Nevertheless, your ophthalmologist might consider creating a capsular window if severe capsule clouding and vision loss are evident.

VASCULAR DISEASE CAUSED BY DIABETES

Diabetics are notorious for developing vascular complications and circulatory disturbances. Chronic uncontrolled high blood sugar levels can promote abnormal blood vessel formation in the outflow drain system of the eye. The vascular disorder can eventually reduce fluid drainage from the eye resulting in glaucoma. Glaucoma is a very serious complication, and it will cause pain and permanent loss of vision if it cannot be controlled.

Vascular changes occur in the retinal blood vessels of diabetic dogs, but clinical diabetic retinopathy as occurs in humans is extremely rare in diabetic dogs. However, dogs with high blood lipids (cholesterol, triglyceride, etc.) can develop xanthogranulomas in the retinas prior to or after cataract surgery. If granulomas occur, the diet must be strictly controlled, and additional medications may be prescribed.

Diabetic dogs often have abnormally high cholesterol and triglycerides (fats) in their blood. The high blood fat levels cause inflammation and damage to the cells lining the blood vessels. The inflammation can cause spontaneous hemorrhage into any body tissue including the brain (stroke), eye (hyphema), kidney, bladder, skin, and etc. The fats also predispose the blood cells to rupturing (hemolysis) when blood samples are collected. Hemolysis, or rupturing of the red blood cells, can artificially increase fructosamine test levels by up to 150%. Several blood chemistry test values are altered when high cholesterol or high triglycerides are present, and this can complicate interpretation of the test results by the veterinarian.

Inadequate insulin in the blood contributes to creating viscous cycles. As fats stores break down (lipolysis), the fat products accumulate in the blood (hyperlipidemia). Hyperlipidemia can lead to falsely lowered fructosamine levels and impair kidney function[5]. The increased fats (lipids) in blood can affect the eyes. When inflammation occurs in the eyes, the strict filtering process associated with formation of aqueous can be altered, allowing lipids, blood cells, and proteins to contaminate the aqueous. The lipid contamination causes a cloudy eye because of clouding of the aqueous. This contaminated fluid is potentially able to plug the drain system and cause secondary glaucoma. Continued high blood fat levels can cause gradual accumulation of fat in the cornea resulting in clouding of the cornea and vision impairment.

MANY INSULIN PRODUCTS ARE AVAILABLE FOR DIABETICS (APPENDIX II)

Vetsulin (known as Caninsulin® outside the US) had been used worldwide by veterinarians for more than 20 years. Due to a manufacturing issue, actions were taken in November 2009 in the US to limit availability of the existing Vetsulin inventory. Once the inventory was exhausted, Vetsulin was unavailable until the issue was resolved. During the time off the market, Merck updated the manufacturing process and re-qualified Vetsulin with the FDA. The only change in Vetsulin was to change the labeled ratio of amorphous insulin to crystalline insulin from 30:70 to 35:65. This ratio change more accurately reflected the average ratio range during shelf life. Vetsulin was re-introduced to the US market in April 2013. Vetsulin continues to be an excellent product with uncompromised safety. Vetsulin is the only FDA approved insulin for use in dogs and cats.

Vetsulin is purified pork derived insulin for use in diabetic dogs and cats from Merck Animal Health. Pork insulin has a similar amino acid structure to normal canine insulin, and it usually provides a good therapeutic response. Dogs with known allergies to pork products should be observed for signs of immune reactions when beginning this insulin therapy. Local allergic reactions include temporary redness, itchy, and hardening of the injection site. The site may look like a mosquito bite. More generalized allergic reactions to pork can be mild and include an onset of a skin rash or hives, itchy skin, vomiting and diarrhea, or the signs may be more severe and include sudden weakness, choking, and difficulty breathing. Emergency treatment with antihistamines and corticosteroids are needed if a severe pork allergy occurs.

Insulin derived from cows is closest to insulin naturally found in cats, so bovine insulin is often prescribed for diabetic cats.

Human insulin is manufactured in laboratories using DNA recombinant technology. It is identical to human insulin derived from the normal human pancreas. **Human insulin can be safely administered to diabetic dogs.** Prior to the new processes for manufacturing human insulin, beef and beef-pork derived insulin were used in treating human diabetics. Beef and beef-pork combination insulin products were discontinued for human use in the United States because of the risk for contamination with mad cow disease organisms.

Protamine zinc insulin (PZI) is a beef or beef-pork insulin still available in some countries. Protamine is a protein extracted from salmon. When protamine is combined with zinc, it slows absorption of insulin. PZI insulin has been available through compounding pharmacies using human insulin. This compounded product can be excellent for treating diabetic dogs, but inconsistencies in quality have been a problem in some situations.

Diabetic dogs vary in their response to insulin treatment, and your pet may require a certain type of insulin to achieve satisfactory control of diabetes while another dog might require a different type of insulin. Each diabetic dog is an individual, and more than one type of insulin might be recommended for trial until ideal control of diabetes has been achieved.

Injectable insulin cannot be given as an oral medication because the enzymes in the stomach will destroy insulin before it can be utilized.

Many insulin products are available, and they vary as to time of onset and duration of action. Combinations of short and long acting insulins are available. Consult your veterinarian prior to changing insulin types or dosing.

Always verify that you have obtained the correct insulin and matching syringes prior to using the insulin and syringes. Dispensing errors can cause serious complications for your pet.

Insulin is labeled U-40, U-100, and U-500. The "U" delineates the number of units per milliliter (ml) or cubic centimeter (cc) of fluid in the insulin vial. It is extremely important to verify the syringe matches the number of insulin units in the vial. Using the wrong syringe can result in a very dangerous and improper dose of insulin being injected into your pet.

Do not rely on the color-coding of the packaging or needle cover to evaluate the syringes. Some syringes for U-40 insulin have a red cover and a red scale, but some U-40 syringes have orange covers and black scales. Syringes for use with U-100 usually have an orange needle cover and a black scale on the syringe. Carefully examine the syringe and be certain it is proper for the insulin you are administering.

Insulin pens are all U-100. This is standardized worldwide; however, insulin pens are not commonly used for treating dogs.

A variety of insulin syringes and needles are manufactured including 1 ml, 1/2 ml, and 3/10 ml sizes. The 3/10 is for 30 unit doses or less; the ½ ml is for 50 unit doses or less. The 1 ml is for 100 units or less. The insulin needles vary in length and thickness. Needles are 12.7 mm long (about ½ inch) or 8 mm long (5/16"). Diameter of the needles is measured in gauges, with higher numbers indicating smaller diameters. Needles are available in 28 gauge and in the smaller 30 gauge sizes. BD also manufactures an ultra fine short needle with 31-gauge 8 mm (5/16") length.

Intervet manufactures a U-40 (1/2 ml) syringe with a 29 gauge ½" in length for use with Vetsulin. **Dogs with thick skin and long hair are more easily treated with longer needles; the longer needles do not cause more discomfort when injecting the insulin.**

Syringes should not be reused or prefilled. Syringes and needles should be properly disposed of to prevent injury and/or misuse. Your community will have recommendations on safe disposal of used syringes and needles. Syringes and needles cannot be reused or recycled.

INJECTING INSULIN

The preferred injection sites for dogs are along the top of the neck and back down to the hips. The entire area can be utilized for injecting insulin. This area has a layer of fat below the skin, and it has less sensory nerves than other skin surfaces. The lower concentration of sensory nerve endings reduces the chance for injection discomfort. The neck skin is often thicker, so care must be given to inject the insulin properly.

The insulin should be injected in the subcutaneous fat; this is just below the skin, rather than into the skin. If you inject too deeply and enter muscle, the injection will be painful, and the insulin could be absorbed too quickly. This might result in a shorter than necessary insulin action.

If the injection is not deep enough, it will penetrate into the skin and not through the skin. The insulin will be poorly absorbed from the skin. Incomplete injection or complete penetration as occurs with a through and through skin penetration prevents insulin from being useful. A wet area will develop at the injection site if the injection is through and through the skin. Dogs with long hair coats are prone to poor injection techniques. Shaving the hair along the back or a patch on the back can be helpful when first learning how to inject insulin. The hair can be parted with a comb or brush to expose the skin surface.

Pick up a fold of skin and insert the needle at a 45-90-degree angle. Hold the pinch and inject the insulin. Release the skin pinch and remove the needle from the skin. The skin should not be wiped with alcohol or any chemicals prior to injection, but the injection should not be given in an area of obvious dermatitis, skin cysts, wound, or matted hair.

The insulin injection site should be rotated between 6-8 areas from the neck and down the back. This will prevent injecting into the same area every day, and it will reduce the risks for developing scars that can interrupt absorption of the insulin.

Insulin injections should provide minimal discomfort. Occasionally an injection will cause a slight discomfort, but this should be a rare occurrence. Rarely, a small drop of blood will be noticed at the injection site. This is not important, and it can be wiped away with a moist cloth or paper towel. Some dogs are less tolerant of cold insulin injections, and warming to room temperature prior to injecting is acceptable.

ESTABLISHING THE DOSE FOR INSULIN TREATMENTS

The initial dose for insulin is an estimate based upon general body condition, size of patient, and blood glucose levels. Twice daily injections are generally recommended along with special diets. Your pet's veterinarian will guide you in establishing a proper dose and type of insulin for your pet. An initial dose of 0.25 unit of insulin per pound of bodyweight (up to 0.5 unit per pound in large dogs) can be a starting point, but long acting insulins may require lower doses. Also, metabolism differences in dogs will vary the duration of insulin activity in individual dogs, and repeated blood glucose testing will be necessary to find the optimum dose. The initial insulin dose should be given for 5-7 days; thereafter, the dose can be adjusted every 3-4 days as needed. Changes in the insulin dose should be made in 10% increments.

A blood glucose range between 90-216 mg/dl during a 24-hour period would be ideal. Blood glucose levels are determined by glucose curve testing.

WHAT IS A GLUCOSE CURVE?

Glucose curve techniques vary. In most instances, the dog is hospitalized, and the first blood sample is taken prior to feeding and insulin injection. Then feeding and administration of the prescribed insulin dose are permitted. Blood samples are taken every two hours until the glucose concentration has crossed the nadir or lowest glucose level in the curve. After the nadir the glucose level will begin to increase. The Nadir is usually expected to occur about six hours after the insulin

(Humulin N ®, Novolin N, Vetsulin) has been administered, but individual variations occur. Hourly testing may be recommended if the Somogyi effect is suspected (page 44). If possible, 24 hour testing is recommended for more accurate information. Ideal glucose curves will reduce blood glucose to between 90-200 mg/dl during most of the time between insulin injections. Slight hyperglycemia or hypoglycemia can be acceptable if clinical signs do not suggest problems (polyuria/polydipsia, weight loss, appetite loss, etc). Day-to-day variations will occur with serial blood glucose curve testing, so it is important to assess the whole patient and not change insulin doses just because the glucose curve has moderate changes[8].

Hospitalized dogs can have irregular or poor test data during glucose curve testing as a result of hospital-induced stress. The owner may need to take the pet from the clinic and return for each timed sample. Even with outpatient blood testing, stress can be an important factor in obtaining valid data.

Veterinarians often recommend beginning the glucose curve two hours after the initial feeding and insulin injections at home, then testing the blood glucose every two hours during an 8-hour period. This shortened glucose curve can provide excellent clinical information. It also reduces the stress and allows the pet to eat a normal meal and receive insulin prior to the stress event of blood testing and hospitalization. Obtaining valid data can be a challenging problem for the owner and veterinarian. However, all parameters are involved in assessing the level of control in the diabetic patient. Accurate logs and medical records with dates, times, insulin doses, feeding, patient weight, and overall health all contribute to the final evaluation.

Single Blood sample testing for glucose can be taken at the time expected for the glucose nadir (lowest expected level). The time for testing is based upon previous glucose curve data, but it can be variable and not necessarily accurate. Blood tests for glucose can vary by 15%, so some variability should be expected when testing on a regular basis. Unusual test results should be verified by repeated testing.

Hand held portable blood glucose meters are accurate when calibrated for use in dogs[9, 10]. Glucose meters require a drop of fresh blood. Blood can be collected from the lip, earflap, tail head, toenail, or callus (elbow). Blood collection can be difficult because it might cause pain, and your pet may not tolerate this event. However, if you are able to collect blood, the glucose meter will give you an advantage in monitoring your diabetic pet[11-13].

The owner must be responsible and be able to monitor and record the response to treatments. Particular attention should be given to the following: water consumption, urination, appetite, attitude, and either weight loss or gain.

Stable patients with well-controlled diabetes should have follow up examinations every 3 months to assess general health.

Blood glucose curves are used to adjust the glucose dose. Urine glucose and urine ketone monitoring can be helpful in identifying when a glucose curve should be evaluated.

Urine glucose testing for glucose can be beneficial in detecting hyperglycemia in a stable diabetic patient. Urine testing will detect ketones. Urine test results should not be considered reliable for adjusting insulin dosing; blood glucose curves are necessary to evaluate the response to insulin.

If a diabetic dog does not eat a meal, 1/3 of the insulin dose can be administered. If one half of the normal meal is eaten, then ½ of the usual insulin dose can be given. If ¾ of the normal meal is consumed, ¾ of the normal insulin can be given. If the pet continues to have a poor appetite, your veterinarian should examine the pet immediately.

INSULIN STORAGE AND UTILIZATION

Insulin generally will be suitable for use for one month after beginning use of the vial when stored at room temperature. Do not freeze insulin. Exposure to direct sunlight and heat can damage the insulin.

If stored in a refrigerator, unopened vials are good until the expiration date. Opened bottles in the refrigerator should be used within 30 days or after 100 injections. The insulin vials used for dogs requiring small doses of insulin will acquire more punctures in the rubber stopper, and the risk for contamination of the vial increases with each puncture.

If the insulin becomes discolored, the texture changes, or the rubber stopper leaks or breaks off into the vial, the vial should be replaced with a new vial.

Write the date on the bottle when you begin using it. Finish each bottle before using another bottle. Keeping more than one bottle as active sources for insulin is wasteful.

Discard your insulin if you do not get the desired response. Begin using a new vial of insulin; if the response is still not proper, consult your veterinarian.

REASONS FOR INSULIN
TREATMENT FAILURES

A variety of issues can cause poor control of diabetes including the following: (1) poor injection technique, (2) improper syringe/dosing, (3) poor quality insulin, (4) poor diet management, (5) medication containing glucocorticoids, (6) medications containing insulin antagonists, (7) chronic infections, (8) pancreatitis, (9) hypothyroidism, (10) neoplasia, (11) hormone imbalance, (12) lipemia, (13) antibody formation, and (14) hyperadrenocorticism (Cushing's disease/syndrome).

1. Poor injection techniques result in inadequate insulin being absorbed. Dogs with long hair may need to have the injection sites clipped periodically to be certain the needle penetrates completely through the skin and into the subcutaneous tissues. The insulin injection site should be rotated to prevent lipodystrophy and poor absorption of the insulin. If the same site is used for injections, changes in the subcutaneous fat can affect insulin absorption. This could cause blood glucose levels to be abnormally higher or lower than expected.

2. The correct needle and syringe must be used to insure administration of a proper dose of insulin. Always verify new needles and insulin vials as the correct ones you use for your pet.

3. The insulin must be properly stored and open vials of insulin should be discarded each month. Outdated insulin or insulin left in a hot or sunny location can become inactive and useless. Changes in the appearance of the insulin caused by chemical breakdown or deterioration will inactive insulin. Contamination of the insulin vial by leakage from

the rubber stopper can inactivate the insulin. If a sudden problem arises when a new bottle of insulin is utilized, the bottle should be discarded and replaced with a new bottle of insulin. While it is uncommon, insulin can be damage during shipping to the vendor, and the insulin could be rendered less effective.

4. Diet regulation and feeding times are very important in routine maintenance. Wide variations in times of insulin administration will increase the risks for hypoglycemia or hyperglycemia. Changes in the diet will alter blood glucose levels. Remember, the best treatment for diabetics involves diet management, regular exercise, feeding time regulation, and regular insulin injections.

5. Medications containing glucocorticoids, i.e. steroids (eye medications, ear medications, skin lotions, skin creams, skin sprays, etc.) will contribute to insulin resistance. **Corticosteroids should be eliminated, reduced, or replaced with non-steroidal anti-inflammatory drugs (NSAIDs) when possible.**

Blood plasma insulin is transported into the brain by insulin binding to blood-brain barrier insulin receptors. Transport occurs through micro vessel endothelial cells. Glucocorticoids (steroids) antagonize insulin receptor action in the brain and peripheral tissues. Dexamethasone (a synthetic steroid) also impairs insulin transport into the brain. **Decreasing insulin transport into the brain will stimulate the appetite, increase fat accumulation, and cause weight gain; therefore, corticosteroids can lead to obesity**[15]. Increasing brain insulin transport reduces food intake and body fat accumulation. Exercise stimulates insulin transport into the brain by improving blood circulation in the brain.

Corticosteroids are available in many medications including the following: eye medications, ear medications, skin medications and lotions, tablets, capsules, and oral liquids. Corticosteroids can be found in combination medications used for topical or oral administration. Natural and homeotherapy medications can contain steroids and chemicals that can interfere with regulation of diabetics just as corticosteroids.

Many dogs have allergies, and the allergies are often treated with corticosteroid oral medication and/or injections. Topical application of corticosteroids (skin ointments, eye ointments or eye drops, ear ointments or drops) can interfere with insulin activity. Topical corticosteroids are more likely to interfere with insulin activity in small dog breeds. The allergy patient with diabetes provides a challenge if corticosteroids are necessary to control the allergy discomfort and signs of disease. If corticosteroids (prednisone, prednisolone, Temaril-P ®, etc) are necessary to control allergy diseases, your veterinarian may recommend larger insulin doses to offset the corticosteroid actions upon insulin.

Always inform your veterinarian about every medication and supplement you give to your diabetic pet. Take all medications and supplements with you when you have your appointment with your veterinarian.

6. Drugs that function as insulin antagonists are uncommonly prescribed, but megestrol acetate and medroxyprogesterone acetate are occasionally utilized for skin or metabolic conditions, and their actions will reduce insulin effectiveness.

7. Diabetic dogs that do not respond to insulin as expected should be evaluated for concurrent diseases. **Infections are probably the most common reason for insulin resistance.** Pets with chronic kidney disease and chronic infections (dental disease[18], skin disease, cystitis, etc.) often require higher than usual insulin doses to control diabetes. Stress, infections (urinary tract infections, ear infections, skin pyoderma, etc), and obesity can lead to loss of insulin effectiveness. Dental disease with endodontic infections can interfere with regulation of blood glucose[18]. Particular care and monitoring of your pet's teeth and gums are necessary in diabetics. Saliva with higher than normal glucose levels encourages bacteria to reside in the mouth and gums, predisposing the pet to serious dental disease. Infections in the mouth can easily spread to other parts of the body resulting in complications. Regular dental examinations, teeth cleaning, and treating decayed teeth are important.

8. Chronic pancreatitis occurs commonly in diabetic dogs, but it is not always recognized as an active disease process. A thorough examination

of the pancreas including imaging and laboratory testing should be performed to verify pancreatitis is not present.

9. Hypothyroidism (euthyroid sick syndrome) can be caused by unregulated diabetes. Testing for total thyroxin (T4), free T4 concentration, and thyroid-stimulating hormone concentration would be recommended prior to administering thyroid supplementation. Nevertheless, a few dogs with primary hypothyroidism will have normal laboratory test values, and they are difficult to diagnose.

10. Tumors of any type could stimulate inflammation and/or produce products that interfere with insulin. A general physical examination including imaging of the chest and abdomen should be considered at the onset of diabetes, and particularly if the patient has insulin resistance.

11. Insulin resistance occurs with natural hormone production or administration of hormones[16, 17]. Progesterones or estrogens should not be given to diabetic dogs. Normally produced progesterone in bitches recently in estrus can complicate regulation of the diabetic dog. Diabetic female dogs should be spayed to prevent hormonal complications in regulating diabetes.

12. Insulin resistance also occurs in dogs with elevated blood triglycerides (fats). Dogs with hyperlipidemia will have very high cholesterol and triglyceride concentrations, and this could be related to insulin-resistance. It is common to find elevated lipids in miniature schnauzer dogs, and this could be an inherited lipid disorder. In dogs with high lipid values and proper low-fat high-fiber diets, the addition of gemfibrozil or niacin might aid in reducing lipid in the blood.

13. The chemical structure of insulin amino acid subunits varies among species. An individual can develop antibodies to insulin, and treatment with insulin could cause an allergic reaction. Nevertheless, allergic reactions to insulin are rare. Porcine insulin should be administered with care to dogs with known allergies to pork. Beef derived insulin given to dogs usually results in antibody production. Insulin antibody formation is common when beef derived or human insulin is administered to dogs. Fortunately, antibodies to insulin do not commonly seem to affect glycemic control in diabetic dogs; however, antibodies can potentially

reduce the effectiveness of insulin. Antibody production might require the diabetic to receive higher than usual insulin doses.

14. Diabetic dogs are commonly affected with Cushing's disease or Cushing's syndrome, and diabetes will be difficult to regulate if the Cushing's process is not controlled. Cushing's Disease is caused by excessive pituitary gland secretion of adrenocorticotropin (ACTH). This is often the result of a tumor or hyperplasia of the pituitary gland. Pituitary tumors cause 80-85% of the cases of Cushing's disease in dogs. The excess ACTH stimulates the production and release of the hormone cortisol. Cortisol has many functions, and it aids in regulating the use of protein, fats, and carbohydrates.

Cushing's Syndrome has similar clinical features to Cushing's disease. Cushing's syndrome can be caused by chronic and/or excessive use of corticosteroids (iatrogenic Cushing's or Cushing's medicomentosus). Hyperadrenocorticism can result from neoplasms of the adrenal cortex. Adrenal cortex tumors are functional and secrete cortisol independent of ACTH stimulation. Adrenal tumors cause 15-20% of the cases.

Abnormally high levels of cortisol production by the adrenal glands cause Cushing's disease. Cortisol is the major natural glucocorticoid secreted by the adrenal cortex, and it affects glucose, protein and fat metabolism. This results in high insulin requirements in diabetic dogs.

The common signs of diabetes (increased thirst and urination, weight gain/loss, pendulous abdomen, poor hair coat with hair loss on the trunk, excessive panting, thin skin, muscle wasting, lethargy, etc.) can be totally attributed to Cushing's disease. Dogs with Cushing's disease might have elevated blood glucose, but the glucose can return to normal levels once treatments control Cushing's disease. Laboratory testing often reveals elevated blood cholesterol, triglycerides, alkaline phosphatase, and alanine trasaminase levels.

Cushing's disease and Cushing's syndrome are primarily diagnosed based upon the clinical signs. Nevertheless, laboratory tests including ACTH stimulation, low dose dexamethasone suppression, and urinary cortisol/ creatinine testing are helpful. Abdominal sonography can aid in finding adrenal gland tumors. MRI can aid in finding pituitary tumors.

Dogs with diabetes and Cushing's disease usually need medications to control both diseases. Nevertheless, Cushing's disease is one of the most complicated endocrine disorders, and it can be very difficult to diagnose.

Despite the above reasons for treatment failures, dogs are occasionally encountered that seem to metabolize the insulin too quickly or at an uneven rate. In these select patients it may be worthwhile to consider administering a "background insulin" once each day in addition to the routine insulin. An example would be to administer glargine or detemir once each day at the same time the regular Lente insulin is administered. This type of dual treatment is reserved for the few dogs that cannot be regulated by traditional methods, and when all other reasons for insulin failure have been exhausted.

Regardless of the concurrent disease or techniques responsible for insulin resistance, when the problem is resolved, the insulin dose must be reduced to prevent a hypoglycemia episode. For example, if a dog has a urinary tract infection or hypothyroidism, and the conditions respond to medical therapy, insulin could become more effective, and a lowered dose may be all that is necessary to control blood glucose levels. Failure to consider this "new" response to the insulin dose could result in "over-dosing" and hypoglycemia.

MANAGING THE UNCOMPLICATED DIABETIC

Diabetic dogs are generally considered well controlled when the signs of diabetes have been restricted. The well-controlled diabetic dog does not have classic signs of diabetes such as uncontrolled water intake and frequent urination[13]. Maintenance of body weight is important. Weight gain or loss will alter the necessary insulin requirement. Overweight dogs that developed diabetes and subsequently lost weight should not be permitted to regain excess weight. Periodic glucose curve testing and fructosamine testing values will provide additional information about diabetes control. Nevertheless, most diabetic dogs are not tightly controlled; many remain mildly hyperglycemic.[14] Precise control of diabetes would be ideal, but this may be beyond the owner's capabilities for a variety of reasons including individual dog physiology and response to insulin injections.

Motivated owners with the ability to monitor their pet throughout the day may be able to gain better control of blood glucose levels by daily blood and urine testing. Glucose meters calibrated for dogs can provide accurate data[11]. Owners using routine blood tests should chart their findings and keep a detailed log of when the testing was performed and how long after the insulin injection was given.

REGULAR EXERCISE IS BENEFICIAL FOR DIABETIC DOGS

Diabetic dogs like diabetic humans benefit from regular exercise. A routine of daily exercise, even strenuous exercise will be beneficial in lowering blood glucose levels. However, occasional strenuous exercise (weekend warrior syndrome) can complicate blood glucose regulation.

FRUCTOSAMINE

Fructosamine is a blood protein commonly used for monitoring diabetics. Fructosamine is a marker of mean or average blood glucose concentration. Fructosamine is not affected by stress. Blood glucose binds to proteins and produces fructosamine. The fructosamine test is a single measurement that reflects the average glucose concentration during the previous 2-3 weeks, based upon the half-life of plasma proteins. Single fructosamine samples should be evaluated in concert with the general health of the patient. Treated diabetic dogs can have short-term episodes of hypoglycemia or hyperglycemia not detected by fructosamine testing.

FRUCTOSAMINE RANGES FOR DOGS

NORMAL NON-DIABETIC	225-365
NEWLY DIAGNOSED DIABETIC	320-850
EXCELLENT CONTROL WITH INSULIN	300-350
GOOD CONTROL WITH INSULIN	350-400
FAIR CONTROL WITH INSULIN	400-450
POOR CONTROL WITH INSULIN	>450
PROLONGED HYPOGLYCEMIA	<250

Dogs with hypoalbuminemia will have decreased fructosamine levels, and this would be considered a false negative test result.

Many diabetic dogs have elevated blood cholesterol and triglyceride levels. Blood samples collected from these dogs frequently have hemolysis or rupturing of the blood cells during the collection process. Blood samples with hemolysis tested for fructosamine will usually have falsely elevated fructosamine levels. Hemolysis can cause a 150% increase in fructosamine levels. Hemolysis can be very difficult to avoid in diabetic patients, but using large gauge needles when collecting blood and collecting blood from large veins such as the jugular vein can reduce hemolysis. Minimal suction on the syringe during the collection process will reduce rupturing blood cells. All that being said, I have found it very difficult to collect non-hemolyzed blood from my own diabetic dog!

KETONES AND KETOACIDOSIS

Ketones are a normal byproduct of fat breakdown in the healthy body. Ketone levels rise during periods of fasting or when high protein diets are administered over time (Atkins Diet[20]). The rise in ketones is much more dramatic in humans than in dogs. Ketoacidosis is a serious metabolic complication of diabetes. When insulin is not present in the body, glucose cannot be used for supplying energy because the glucose simply cannot get into the cells to feed the cells energy. Therefore, fats are broken down to provide an alternative source for energy. However, rapid fat breakdown produces high levels of ketones. Electrolyte imbalance (sodium, potassium, etc.) in the blood and acidosis coexist with ketosis. The dog with ketoacidosis is generally sick with a poor appetite and weakness. Vomiting can occur. Dogs with ketosis often have a "sweet odor" to their breath. Ketones will spill into the urine, and they can easily be detected with urine dipstick tests. Ketoacidosis develops in undiagnosed diabetic dogs. However, under dosing with insulin, insulin resistance, obesity, medications, and diseases can complicate diabetes and cause ketoacidosis.

Ketoacidosis can be a severe medical emergency. Intensive care utilizing intravenous fluids and rapid acting insulin may be necessary to stabilize the sick dog. Blood electrolyte concentrations and acid-base balance must be achieved quickly to prevent severe complications and death.

HYPOGLYCEMIA

Hypoglycemia occurs when blood glucose levels are too low, generally less than 90 mg/dl. Most dogs will not show signs of hypoglycemia until glucose levels drop to 50 mg/dl or lower. Clinical signs of hypoglycemia include weakness, staggering (ataxia), disorientation, restlessness, shivering, hunger, convulsions, and death.

Hypoglycemia can be caused because by insulin over dosage (wrong insulin, wrong syringe, or improper measurement of insulin in syringe).

Injecting insulin before eating a meal can result in hypoglycemia if the pet decides not to eat. It is always safer to wait until the meal is consumed before giving the insulin injection. I administer the insulin while my dog is eating.

Excessive exercise can contribute to hypoglycemia. For example, a diabetic dog that stays at home and has a sedentary life during the week cannot be expected to go out and hike all weekend without interfering with normal insulin and glucose relationships.

The diabetic needs a solid routine of eating, regular exercise, and regular insulin injections, or special attention will be necessary with diet and insulin adjustments. Your veterinarian can advise you about changing diets, insulin types, or insulin doses. Insulin should not be administered at the regular dose if your pet is not eating normal food volumes. General recommendations for dogs with poor appetites are as follows: if the pet eats ½ of the normal amount of food, give ½ the usual insulin dose; if the pet eats ¾ of the normal amount of food, give ¾ of the usual insulin dose. However, if the pet does not eat any food, ¼ of the insulin dose can be safely administered. This varying insulin dose should not be the routine method for handling the diabetic. If your pet has a highly variable appetite, further examinations and food trials may become necessary. Consult with your veterinarian.

Hypoglycemia may not cause clinical signs despite low blood glucose levels[19]. The lack of signs of hypoglycemia can be explained by a temporary low blood glucose that improves with the next meal or the blood glucose levels are just slightly low and do not cause visible signs of hypoglycemia.

WHAT TO DO IF YOU CAUSE OR RECOGNIZE HYPOGLYCEMIA SIGNS?

Emergency treatment for hypoglycemia is oral administration of glucose (Karo syrup, maple syrup, or honey) 0.5 gm/pound of bodyweight or approximately enough liquid to moisten the lining of the mouth and tongue. The syrup or honey can be rubbed into the gums and tongue, resulting in rapid absorption of glucose into the blood. Forcing fluids into the mouth of a comatose dog can cause aspiration pneumonia. If your pet does not respond within 10-15 minutes, you must seek medical attention at your veterinarian's office or animal emergency clinic.

Intravenous dextrose can be given: 1-5 ml 50% solution slowly over ten minutes.

Small amounts of food should be fed every 1-2 hours until the overdose has been corrected. The insulin dose may need permanent reduction to prevent recurring episodes of hypoglycemia.

WHAT IS THE SOMOGYI EFFECT?

The Somogyi effect is a rebound hyperglycemia phenomenon. It occurs when blood glucose levels fall too rapidly or fall to less than 90 mg/dl after insulin has been administered. This results in either lethargy and restlessness or increased appetite. The reduced blood glucose stimulates the brain to release adrenaline followed by release of cortisol, glucagon, and growth hormone. The hormones cause blood glucose to rise by gluconeogenesis (a release of glucose from liver glycogen stores). The hormones also increase peripheral resistance to insulin. This secondary elevation in blood glucose causes signs of diabetes such as increased thirst and frequent urination. If the signs are incorrectly thought to be due to insufficient insulin, the dosage of insulin might mistakenly be increased. The increased insulin dose will worsen the chain reaction, until the mechanisms have been depleted resulting in severe hypoglycemia. The Somogyi effect hyperglycemia can persist for as long as three days after a single hypoglycemic event. Thus, the blood glucose levels may not normalize just because the insulin dose has been reduced. A blood glucose curve is the only diagnostic method to confirm a Somogyi effect. The glucose curve will indicate a low glucose nadir (hypoglycemia) followed by a rebound hyperglycemia or a rapid decrease in glucose with an adequate nadir followed by a rebound hyperglycemia. Affected dogs often require insulin doses be reduced by 20%.

WHAT IS THE HYPEROSMOLAR SYNDROME?

Hyperosmolar syndrome is a severe metabolic disaster occurring in chronic uncontrolled diabetics. The affected dog will quickly pass through the classic sign of diabetes and become very weak and depressed. Water and food consumption will be suppressed, and a comatose state will develop very rapidly. Ketoacidosis is not present because the transition into the hyperosmolar syndrome occurs quickly, but blood glucose levels will be very high (>650 mg/dl). The elevated blood glucose levels draw water out of the brain causing coma and death. Aggressive treatment with intravenous fluids and continuous monitoring of blood electrolytes and blood chemistry values (liver function, kidney function, etc) are critical. Nevertheless, the prognosis for dogs with hyperosmolar syndrome is poor. Most die within 24 hours of signs of hyperosmolar syndrome.

NUTRITION AND FEEDING THE DIABETIC DOG

While diet management is crucial to regulate the diabetic, diet alone will not control diabetes in dogs. All diabetic dogs require insulin injections. Finding and maintaining a regular and healthy diet for a diabetic dog can be challenging. In general, the diabetic diet should have low fat, moderate complex carbohydrates, moderately high fiber, and moderately high protein. Diets with approximately 5-15% fat, 45-50% carbohydrates, 10-20% fiber, and 15-18% protein are recommended in feeding diabetic dogs. **Some variations are allowed, but simple sugars should not be present in the food.** Simple sugars to avoid include the following: fructose, high fructose corn syrup, glucose, cane sugar, organic sugar, honey and molasses. Complex carbohydrates are much better than simple sugars for the diabetic patient.

The simplest way to feed a diabetic dog is to feed a prescription diet made for diabetic dogs. A few examples of commercially available diets for diabetic dogs include the following:

Royal Canin produces Diabetic Dog dry meal. Royal Canin Diabetic Diet has the following: crude protein 18%, fat 7.0%, crude fiber 12.6% and moisture 10%. The ingredients include the following: rice, corn, chicken meal, powdered cellulose, corn gluten meal, wheat, chicken fat, rice hulls, etc). This diet food does not contain simple sugars, and the fat content is low. There are 186 calories in each cup of food.

Hills Prescription Diet W/D contains the following: crude protein 15%, fat 6%, and crude fiber 20%. The ingredients include whole grain corn, peanut hulls, chicken by product meal, chicken liver flavor, soybean meal, and powdered cellulose. There are 243 calories in each cup of food.

Hills Prescription Diet R/D has slightly higher protein and fat contents than W/D, but W/D has a higher fiber content than found in R/D.

Purina DCO diet is compounded for diabetics and dogs with colitis. DCO contains the following: crude protein 21%, fat 10%, carbohydrates 46%, and moisture 12%.

DIET AND FIBER

Fiber is the non-digestible portion of plants consumed in the diet. Fiber includes cell wall components such as cellulose, hemicelluloses, pectin, and lignin. Also included are intracellular components such as polysaccharides (gums and mucilage)[21.]

Dietary fiber had been classified as either soluble or insoluble fiber in order to distinguish how fiber affected digestion and food absorption. More recently, this classification has been discarded because **many foods contain both soluble and insoluble fibers**. Fiber is also evaluated as to rate of fermentation in the digestive tract. Rapidly fermenting fiber tends to act as soluble fiber, mixing with water and forming a gelatinous mass. Slowly fermenting fiber is generally more insoluble and more effective in adding bulk to the stool. Bulk increases passage of stool through the digestive tract. Most diets contain rapidly and slowly fermenting fiber sources. A brief discussion about fiber will help explain the benefits of fiber in a diabetic dog's diet.

Soluble fiber is beneficial because it attracts water and forms a gelatinous mass in the stomach and intestines. The gelatinous mass mixes with nutrients and slows emptying of the stomach. This helps maintain a feeling of fullness and reduces hunger, thus there is less desire to eat. The absorption of nutrients from the gelatinous mass is slowed, reducing the concentration of carbohydrates and fat absorbed into the intestines and into the blood. Dogs fed diets with 12% to 21% crude fiber consumed less metabolizable energy than dogs fed low fiber diets[22]. Fiber will bind with bile acids, and the bile will pass into the feces with the fiber. The loss of bile acids can stimulate the liver to produce more bile acids from cholesterol, thereby reducing cholesterol levels in the body. Fiber balances intestinal pH, stimulates intestinal fermentation, and increases production of short-chain fatty acids. Fatty acids stimulate glucose transport into the intestinal mucosa (lining) and regulation of glucose absorption in the intestine. Fatty acids help stabilize blood glucose levels by action on pancreatic insulin release and liver control of glycogen breakdown. This prevents a rapid rise in blood glucose and reduces blood glucose swings. Short chain fatty acids also reduce cholesterol production by the liver.

Soluble fibers are found in legumes (peas, soybeans, other beans), oats, oat bran, rolled oats, whole oat flour, oat rim, whole grain barley, dry milled barley, psyllium husk, rye, barley, root vegetables like potatoes, broccoli, carrots, and onions.

Insoluble fiber does not dissolve in water, and it passes through the entire digestive tract unchanged. Insoluble fiber adds a satisfying feeling or a feeling of fullness even though fewer calories are absorbed. Insoluble fiber adds bulk to the stool and improves bowel emptying. Insoluble fibers are found in whole grains (wheat, corn, bran), potato skins, flax seeds, and lignins (flax seed, sesame seed, rye, wheat, oat, barley, pumpkin seed, soybeans, broccoli, beans, and some berries). Other sources of insoluble fiber include the following: celery, green beans, tomatoes, cauliflower, fruit, vegetable skins, and seeds and nuts. But, seeds and nuts are often high in fat and not good sources of insoluble fiber for diabetic dogs.

Flax seed and sesame seed are among the highest known sources of lignins. The principal lignin precursor found in flaxseed is secoisolariciresinol diglucoside. Other sources of lignins include cereals (rye, wheat, oat, barley—rye being the richest source), pumpkin seed, soybeans, broccoli, beans, and some berries

Fiber is an important ingredient in the diet, and diabetics benefit from all sources of fiber. However, too much fiber can reduce nutrient absorption, increase weight loss, and cause soft stools, even diarrhea. Dogs with thin body condition should not be encouraged to lose weight by use of high fiber diets. Dogs fed moderate carbohydrate, moderate fat, and high fiber will lose weight, and plasma cholesterol and plasma triglycerides will be lower than if fed regular diets[22].

GOOD FOODS

Good foods include the following meats: lean ground beef, chicken, turkey, duck (no skin or fat in bird meat), lamb, buffalo, venison, tuna in water and other fish, poached or scrambled eggs, low salt broth (beef or chicken), and Campbell's chicken noodle soup.

Low sugar vegetables useful in feeding diabetic dogs include the following: pearl barley, brown rice, celery, green beans, spinach, broccoli, cauliflower, green or red sweet peppers, turnips, carrots (in moderation), tofu, and garlic.

Other useful foods include the following: cooked pasta in moderation, oatmeal, yeast, bran, cottage cheese, and low fat cheese.

LESS DESIRABLE FOODS

Less desirable foods include the following: excess carrots or peas (sugar content too high).

Soft or semi-moist foods often contain simple sugars, and the combination of moisture and sugar promotes a rapid rise in blood glucose.

BAD FOODS

Foods to avoid include all forms of simple sugars including the following: high fructose corn syrup, fructose, maltose, maple syrup, cane sugar, cane molasses, molasses, brown sugar, organic sugar, malt syrup, and dextrose. Avoid giving any candy, chocolate, ice cream, cookies and donuts.

Avoid most commercially available dog treats (read the label and avoid treats with bad contents). Avoid fatty dog treats such as pig ears, jerky treats, rawhide chews, and any form of supplemental animal fats.

SUPPLEMENTS

A multiple vitamin mineral supplement should be given each day.

Supplementation with chromium picolinate and/or cinnamon (pinch up to ½ teaspoon each day) has been beneficial to some diabetic dogs, because the supplements help mobilize insulin.

Other individual ingredients suggested to help certain diabetics include supplementation with one or more of the following: magnesium, antioxidant vitamins (vitamins A, C, and E), selenium, alphalipoic acid, vinegar, and fenugreek.

Fenugreek has been shown to reduce fasting blood glucose[23]. Cholesterol and triglycerides were also reduced when humans ingested 50 grams of fenugreek seed powder[23].

Poorly controlled diabetics characterized by weight loss, altered fat metabolism, ketosis, and liver disorders can benefit from diet supplementation with carnitine. Carnitine is used in metabolism of palmitic and stearic acids. It is also useful in treating myopathies.

Dogs with hyperlipidemia will have high cholesterol and triglyceride concentrations, and this could be related to insulin-resistance. It is common to find elevated lipids in miniature schnauzer dogs, and this might be an inherited lipid disorder. In dogs with high lipid values and proper low-fat high-fiber diets, the addition of gemfibrozil or niacin might aid in reducing lipid in the blood.

Hypothyroidisms can also cause lipid metabolism problems. Furthermore, hypothyroidism can be related to insulin resistance[26].

Omega-3 fatty acid supplements can help reduce blood lipid levels in some individuals

DIACYLGLYCEROL (DAG) AND TRIACYLGLYCEROL (TAG)

DAG and TAG are acylglycerols found in edible vegetable oils including the following: cottonseed oil, palm oil, olive oil, and sesame seed oil. Few studies have been conducted in dogs using DAG and TAG as supplements, but DAG might be effective in helping control appetite, blood fat levels, and fat storage.

GLYCEMIC INDEX

The glycemic index measures a food's impact on blood glucose. The glycemic index compares the speed glucose enters the blood after eating a specific food. Pure glucose has been assigned a value of 100, and foods are compared to this standard. High glycemic foods should be avoided. For example white bread has a high glycemic index of 70. Kidney beans have a low glycemic index of 27. High glycemic index foods include foods such as the following: white bread, baked potatoes, instant rice, low-fiber cereals, and baked goods.

Low glycemic index foods include the following: fruits, vegetables, whole and minimally processed grains, and legumes. Carrots have a glycemic index of 71, but sweet potatoes are only 54.

In general, processed foods have higher glycemic index than non-processed foods.

The glycemic index might be listed on the food product: low glycemic index would be 55 or less; medium glycemic index levels would be 56-69, and high glycemic index levels are over 70.

If a diabetic must be fasted because of disease or test requirements, the insulin dose can be administered at ½ the normal dose. This will prevent ketoacidosis and severe complications caused by immediate cessation of insulin treatments, and the lower dose has minimal risks for causing serious hypoglycemia.

DOGS AS SENTINALS FOR HUMAN DIABETICS PATIENTS

Dogs can recognize and respond to type 1 diabetic humans when hypoglycemia is developing in the human diabetic. Alerted dogs respond by exhibiting unusual or anxious behavior including vocalizing, licking the owner, nuzzling, and jumping on the owner. Intense staring, trembling by the responsive pet and signs of fear also suggested a hypoglycemic event in the diabetic owner. It is not known how dogs can sense the hypoglycemic episode in the diabetic human[27]. Diabetic humans can use their pet as a sentry to alert them about a hypoglycemic event.

DEFINITIONS

ACTH: Adrenocorticotropic hormone; produced in the pituitary gland as part of the feedback mechanism to stimulate the adrenal gland release of cortisol.

ACTH Stimulation test: A test to evaluate adrenal gland function. A small amount of ACTH is injected into the patient; this will stimulate the adrenal glands to release cortisol into the blood. The blood cortisol level can be measured. This test is the primary test for adrenal gland insufficiency.

Cataract: abnormal clouding of the lens and/or lens capsule.

Cortisol/creatinine ratio: urine testing to determine if an excessive amount of cortisol is present. The urinary cortisol/creatinine ratio is usually elevated in dogs with Cushing's disease.

Cushing's Disease: A disease of the adrenal gland cortex (outer layers) causing increased levels of cortisol into the blood.

Diabetes Mellitus (sugar diabetes): a condition when insufficient insulin production occurs; accompanied by impaired carbohydrate, fat, and protein metabolism.

Glaucoma: abnormal elevation in intraocular pressure resulting in atrophy of the optic nerve, blindness, and chronic pain unless controlled.

Glucagon: a hormone secreted by the alpha cells in the pancreas. Glucagon stimulates glycogenolysis in the liver, i.e. breaks down glycogen stored in the liver to release glucose into the blood. Glucagon also stimulates gluconeogenesis and ketogenesis. Glucagon also stimulates insulin release.

Glucose: sugar found in blood.

Glycemic Index: A number scale comparing how fast a food's glucose will enter the blood stream after eating. A value of 100 has been assigned to pure glucose, since it will be absorbed immediately. The higher the number, the more rapid glucose is absorbed.

Glycogen: is the form in which carbohydrates are stored in the liver and muscle tissues; it is often called animal starch.

Glycogenesis: formation of glycogen from blood glucose (carbohydrates).

Glycogenolysis: breakdown of glycogen to glucose to provide energy to the body tissues.

Glyconeogenesis: formation of glycogen from fat or amino acids, not carbohydrates.

Gluconeogenesis: same as glyconeogenesis

Glycosuria: glucose spilling into the urine causing sticky urine; common in uncontrolled diabetes.

Hormone: A chemical secreted by an endocrine gland into the blood.

Insulin: a hormone secreted by the beta cells in the pancreas; insulin allows glucose, amino acids, and fatty acids enter cells. Insulin promotes excess glucose to be stored as glycogen in the liver.

Ketoacidosis: a dangerous condition when high blood glucose levels, low blood insulin levels, and lypolysis occur in diabetics; results in abnormal blood electrolytes balances and can cause death if not corrected.

Ketones: chemicals formed in the process of fat break down (lipolysis); an alternative source for energy when glucose is not available to the cells; often imparting a sweet odor to the breath; easily detected in urine.

Lens Luxation: displacement of the lens; movement from the normal position because of loss of normal ligament support.

Lipolysis: the chemical action of breaking down fat deposits in the body.

Pancreas: a fleshy, glandular tissue closely attached to the duodenal portion of the small intestine. It consists of an endocrine portion that secretes hormones (insulin, glucagon, and somatostatin) into the blood and exocrine portions that secretes enzymes into the intestine that aid in protein digestion.

Polydipsia: abnormal increase in thirst; increased water intake.

Polyuria: abnormal increase in urine production and urination, often uncontrolled urination.

Somatostatin: a hormone secreted by the delta cells in the pancreas. It causes mild inhibition of insulin and glucagon; decreases gut motility and secretion of digestive enzymes. Somatostatin helps prevent wide swings in blood glucose levels.

REFERENCES AND ADDITIONAL READING LIST

[1]Catchpole B, Ristic, JM, Fleeman LM, Davison LJ. Canine diabetes mellitus: can old dogs teach us new tricks? Diabetologia. 05 Oct;48(10)1948-56.

[2]Fleeman, LM, Rand JS. Management of canine diabetes. Vet Clin North Am Small Animal Pract. 2001 Sept;31(5)):855080, vi.)

[3]Kaiyala KJ, Prigeion RL, Kahn SE, Woods SC, Schwartz MW. Obesity induced by a high-fat diet is associated with reduced brain insulin transport in dogs. Diabetes. 2000 Sep;49(9)1525-33.

[4]Rand JS, Fleeman LM, Farrow HA, Appleton DJ, Lederer R. Canine and feline diabetes mellitus: nature or nurture? J Nutr. 2004 Aug;134(8 Suppl):2072S-2080S.

[5]Cullen CL, Ihle SL, Webb AA, McCarville C. Keratoconjunctival effects of diabetes mellitus in dogs. Vet Ophthalmol. 2005 July-Aug;8(4)215-24.

[6]Beam S, Correa MT, Davidson MG. A retrospective-cohort study on the development of cataracts in dogs with diabetes mellitus: 200 cases. Vet Ophthalmol. 1999;2(3):169-172.

[7]Bagley HL 2nd, Lavach JD. Comparison of postoperative phacoemulsification results in dogs with and without diabetes mellitus: 153 cases (1991-1992). J Am Vet Med Assoc. 1994 Oct 15;205(8):1165-9

[8]Fleeman LM, Rand JS. Evaluation of day-to-day variability of serial blood glucose concentration curves in diabetic dogs. J Am vet Med Assoc. 2003 Feb 1:222(3):317-21.

[9]Johnson BM, Fry MM, Flatland B, Kirk CA: Comparison of human portable blood glucose meter, veterinary portable blood glucose meter, and automated chemistry analyzer for measurement of blood glucose concentrations in dogs. J Am Vet Met Assoc. 2009 December 1:235:11, 1309-1313

[10]Cohen TA, Nelson, RW, Kass PH, Christopher MM, Feldman ED: Evaluation of six portable glucose meters for measuring blood glucose concentration in dogs. J Am Vet Met Assoc., 235:3, 276-280, 2009,

[11]Casella M, Wess G, Reusch CE. Measurement of capillary blood glucose concentrations by pet owners: a new tool in the management of diabetes mellitus. J Am Anim Hosp Assoc 2002:38:239-245.

[12]GlucoPet blood glucose monitoring system user manual. Janesville, Wis: Animal Diabetes, 2005.

[13]Bennett N. Monitoring techniques for diabetes mellitus in the dog and the cat. Clin Tech Small Anim Pract. 2002 May; 17(2):65-69.

[14]Labato MA, Manning AM. Management of the uncomplicated canine diabetic. Semin Vet Med Surg (Small Anim). 1997 Nov;12(4):248-58.

[15]Baura GD, Foster DM, Kaivala K, et al. Insulin transport from plasma into the central nervous system is inhibited by dexamethasone in dogs. Diabetes. 1996 Jan;45(1):86-90.

[16]Renauld A, Scaramal JD, Gómez NV, Márquez, AG, Garrido D, Wanke MM. Natural estrous cycle in normal and diabetic bitches. II.)Serum nonesterified fatty aids and serum free glycerol levels during glucose and insulin tests. Acta Physiol Pharmacol ther Latinoam. 1999;49(1):44-56.

[17]Renauld A, von Lawzewitsch I, Pérez RL, Sverdlik R, Agüero A, Foglia VG, Rodriguez RR. Effect of estrogens on blood sugar, serum insulin

and serum free fatty acids, and pancreas cytology in female dogs. Acta Diabetol Lat. 1983 Jan-Mar;20(1):47-56

[18]Van Nice E. Management of multiple dental infections in a dog with diabetes mellitus. J Vet Dent. 2006 Mar;23(1):18-25.

[19]Whitley NT, Drobatz KJ, Panciera DL. Insulin overdose in dogs and cats: 28 cases (1986-1993). J Am Vet Med Assoc. 1997 Aug 1;211(3):326-30.

[20]Atkins RC. Dr. Atkins' New Diet Revolution. First Quill edition published 2002, New York.

[21]Mitushashi Y, Bauer JE: Dietary management of obesity in companion animals via alteration of lipid metabolism. J Am Vet Med Assoc. 2009 December 1:235:11:1292-1300.

[22]Jewell DE, Toll PW. Effects of fiber on food intake in dogs. Vet Clin Nutr 1996;3:115-118.

[23]Sharma RD, Raghuram TC, Rao NS. Effect of fenugreek seeds on blood glucose and serum lipids in type 1 diabetes. Eur J Clin Nutr. 1990 Apr;44(4):301-6.

[25]Fleeman LM, Rand JS, Markwell PJ. Lack of advantage of high-fibre, moderate-carbohydrate diets in dogs with stabilized diabetes. J Small Anim Pract. 2009 Nov;50(11):604-14.

[26]Ford SL, Nelson RW, Feldman EC Niwa D. Insulin resistance in three dogs with hypothyroidism and diabetes mellitus. J Am Vet Met Assoc. 1993, 1:202(9):1478-80
[27]Wells DL, Lawson SW, Siriwardena AN. Canine responses to hypoglycemia in patients with type 1 Diabetes. J Altern Complement Med. 2008 Dec;14(10):1235-41.

[28]Hess RS, Drobatz KJ. Glargine insulin for treatment of naturally occurring diabetes mellitus in dogs. J Am Vet Med Assoc. 2013 Oct 15;243(8):1154-61.

APPENDICES

The following Appendices will give more specific and detailed information for readers interested in particular topics discussed in the general text.

APPENDIX I: DOG BREEDS AND DIABETES

DOG BREED WITH DIABETES	NUMBER OF DOGS WITH DIABETES
LABRADOR	28
LABRADOR RETRIEVER MIX	12
MINIATURE SCHNAUZER	13
STANDARD SCHNAUZER	6
TOY & MINIATURE POODLE	13
STANDARD POODLE	1
AUSTRALIAN SHEPHERD	10
AUSTRALIAN CATTLE DOG	9
BORDER COLLIE	8
ROTTWEILER	7
SCHIPPERKE	7
DACHSHUND	6
MINIATURE PINSCHER	6
BRITTANY SPANIEL	5
GERMAN SHORTHAIRED POINTER	5
SHIH TZU	5
COCKER SPANIEL	5
PUG	5
LHASA APSO	5

YORKSHIRE TERRIER	5
JACK RUSSELL TERRIER	5
SMALL TERRIER MIX	9
MALTESE	4
WESTHIGHLAND WHITE TERRIER	4
GERMAN SHEPHERD DOG	4
SAMOYED	4
CAIRN TERRIER	3
POMERANIAN	3
CHIHUAHUA	3
WELSH CORGI PEMBROKE	3
AMERICAN ESKIMO	3
PIT BULL TERRIER	3
AUSTRALIAN TERRIER	2
BICHON FRISE	2
GOLDEN RETRIEVER	2
ALASKAN HUSKY	2
BRUSSELS GRIFFON	2
MALAMUTE	2
ALASKAN HUSKY	2
BICHON FRISE	2
CHESAPEAKE BAY RETRIEVER	2
BASSETT HOUND	2
JAPANESE AKITA	2
BREEDS WITH ONE CASE OF DIABETES	27

APPENDIX II: TYPES OF INSULIN AVAILABLE

Many insulin products are available from veterinary hospitals and pharmacies. The following list is provided as information only. Your diabetic pet will need insulin therapy. Your veterinarian will be able to determine which product is most likely to provide the insulin you pet requires. Your input and reports will provide valuable information to your veterinarian. Remember, each diabetic is an individual, and the type of insulin recommended will vary from patient to patient.

Rapid—acting insulin or Ultra short-acting insulin Humalog® (Insulin lispro), Novolog® (kusori or insulin aspart, Apidra (Insulin glulisine)

> Insulin lispro, insulin aspart, and insulin glulisine are insulin analogs that are readily absorbed from the injection site which are used to provide a bolus after a meal.

> Soluble insulin and semilente insulin are available for intravenous injection. This type of insulin would not be used as a daily maintenance treatment for diabetic dogs, but it might be useful at a veterinary emergency clinic.
> Onset of action in 5-20 minutes
> Peak of action in 30-90 minutes
> Duration of action is 3-5 hours
> Can be given immediately before a meal; close to body's natural bolus supply, little risk for hypoglycemia
> Clear solution

Short-acting or regular insulin: Humulin R®, Novolin R®

Short-acting insulins are useful in achieving tight control of diabetic dogs that tend to have blood glucose spikes. Owners with the ability to do home blood glucose testing can use this insulin to help control blood glucose levels in pets that spike glucose levels. Caution must be used to prevent hypoglycemia.
Onset of action in 30-60 min
Peak of action in 2-4 hours
Duration of action is 3-8 hours
Clear solution
Should be injected 30-45 min prior to eating

Intermediate-acting insulins:

Neutral Protamine Hagedorn (NPH): Humulin N ®, Novolin N®
Lente insulin—mixtures of 30% amorphous (semilente) and 70% crystalline (ultralente) insulin suspension
Onset of action in 1-4 hours
Peak of action in 4-12
Duration of action is 12-18 hours
Cloudy appearance

Vetsulin (Merck) is an intermediate-acting insulin derived from pork. It is known as Caninsulin outside the U.S. It is a sterile aqueous zinc suspension of purified pork insulin. Vetsulin is the only FDA approved insulin for use in dogs and cats, but not human diabetics. Porcine insulin has a similar amino acid structure to normal canine insulin. Vetsulin has two peaks of action; the first peak occurs 2-6 hours after injection, and the second peak occurs 8-14 hours after injection. The duration of action is 14-24 hours; however, most dogs require twice daily injections to control blood glucose levels. Vetsulin is only available as a U40 (40 units of insulin/ml), and it is easy to calculate the dose using a 0.5 ml syringe.

Cloudy suspension when properly mixed

Shake thoroughly until a uniform milky suspension is formed

Allow foam/bubbles to disperse before filling syringe

Long-acting insulin:

Ultralente insulins (U)—100% crystalline insulin were discontinued in the US.

PZI insulin's—contain protamine and zinc. Protamine zinc insulin (PZI) is a combination of the protein protamine and insulin. Protamine delays absorption of insulin from the injection site, providing more reliable absorption and longer action from the insulin. Protamine can cause poor insulin absorption, and it may not be useful in all patients because of the delayed absorption

PZI Beef insulin is preferred for treating diabetic cats because bovine insulin is very close to feline insulin. PZI Beef insulin can be obtained from compounding pharmacies.

Long-acting basal insulin: Lantus® (Insulin glargine); Levemir®(Insulin detemir)

Glargine and detemir are considered basal insulins and assume to work as background insulin that mimics the constant low output of insulin by a normal pancreas. Both are artificially constructed and genetically modified human insulin that slows their absorption. Glargine and detemir can be useful in treating canine diabetics. A recommended initial dose for glargine insulin is 0.3 units/kg body weight (0.136 units/pound of weight) given twice each day[27].

Onset of action in 1-2 hours
Peak of action in 6-8 hours (detemir); no peak with Glargine
Duration of action is 6-23 hours (insulin detemir) and 24 hours with Glargine
Clear solution

You should not mix insulin types in the same syringe

Different insulins can be used at different times during the day. Using different types of insulin is not usually prescribed for treating diabetic dogs, but exceptional patients may benefit from using more than one type of insulin each day. Consult your veterinarian prior to using more than one type of insulin.

Pre-mixed Human Insulins include the following:

> Humalog Mix 75/25: 75% insulin lispro protamine and 25% insulin lispro
>> Onset 10-15 minutes
>> Peak varies
>> Duration 10-16 hours
>
> Humalog Mix 50/50: 50% insulin lispro protamine and 50% insulin lispro
>> Onset 10-15 minutes
>> Peak Varies
>> Duration 10-16 hours
>
> Humulin Mix 70/30: 70% NPH and 30% Regular
>> Onset 30-60 minutes
>> Peak varies
>> Duration 10-16 hours
>
> Novolin Mix 70/30: 70% NPH and 30% Regular
>> Onset 30-60 minutes
>> Peak varies
>> Duration 10-16 hours
>
> Humulin Mix 50/50: 50% NPH and 50% regular
>> Onset 30-60 minutes
>> Peak varies
>> Duration 10-16 hours
>
> Novolog Mix 70/30: 70% insulin aspart protamine and 30% insulin aspart
>> 5-15 minutes
>> peak varies
>> Duration 10-16 hours

APPENDIX III: THE 450/500 RULE

The 450/500 rule is useful for humans with diabetes, but it has not been studied for use in dogs. This formula provides an estimate as to how much carbohydrate can be taken in the diet each day based upon the insulin dose.

Divide 500 by the total daily dose of insulin. The answer is the grams of carbohydrate that are covered by one unit of insulin=

40 units a day of Humalog into 500 = 12.5 grams of carbohydrate per unit of insulin.

> The 450 rule is similar. 30 unit dose of regular insulin = one unit of insulin for every 15 grams of carbohydrate.

APPENDIX IV: THE INSULIN SENSITIVITY FACTOR

The insulin sensitivity factor has not been studied in dogs. It is used in diabetic humans as an estimate to determine how much each unit of insulin reduces blood glucose levels.

Use the 1500 and 1800 rules to calculate an insulin sensitivity factor. The 1500 rule estimates the point drop in blood glucose in mg/dl for every unit of **regular insulin administered.**

The 1800 rule estimates the point drop in blood glucose in mg/dl for every unit of **rapid-acting insulin** taken.
The calculation is based on all of the units of insulin taken in one day.

Example: a woman takes 15 units of Humalog and 25 units of NPH per day for a total daily insulin dose of 40 units. Reading the Humalog column, her insulin sensitivity factor is 45 mg/dl (1800 divided by 40). Her blood glucose will be lowered by approximately 45 mg/dl for every unit of Humalog she takes.

73539841R00042

Made in the USA
Columbia, SC
12 July 2017